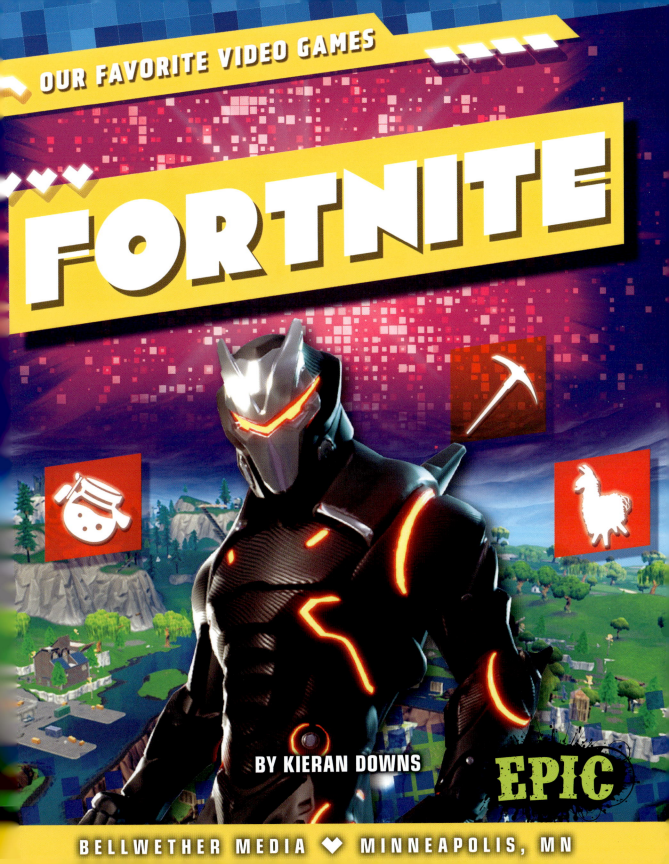

EPIC BOOKS are no ordinary books. They burst with intense action, high-speed heroics, and shadows of the unknown. Are you ready for an Epic adventure?

This is not an official *Fortnite* book. It is not approved by or connected with Epic Games.

This edition first published in 2025 by Bellwether Media, Inc.

No part of this publication may be reproduced in whole or in part without written permission of the publisher. For information regarding permission, write to Bellwether Media, Inc., Attention: Permissions Department, 6012 Blue Circle Drive, Minnetonka, MN 55343.

Library of Congress Cataloging-in-Publication Data

Names: Downs, Kieran, author.
Title: Fortnite / by Kieran Downs.
Description: Minneapolis, MN : Bellwether Media, 2025. | Series: Epic. Our favorite video games | Includes bibliographical references and index. | Audience: Ages 7-12 | Audience: Grades 2-3 | Summary: "Engaging images accompany information about Fortnite. The combination of high-interest subject matter and light text is intended for students in grades 2 through 7"-- Provided by publisher.
Identifiers: LCCN 2024005407 (print) | LCCN 2024005408 (ebook) | ISBN 9798893040456 (library binding) | ISBN 9781644879856 (ebook)
Subjects: LCSH: Fortnite Battle Royale (Game)--Juvenile literature.
Classification: LCC GV1469.35.F67 D68 2025 (print) | LCC GV1469.35.F67 (ebook) | DDC 794.8--dc23/eng/20240205
LC record available at https://lccn.loc.gov/2024005407
LC ebook record available at https://lccn.loc.gov/2024005408

Text copyright © 2025 by Bellwether Media, Inc. EPIC and associated logos are trademarks and/or registered trademarks of Bellwether Media, Inc. Bellwether Media is a division of Chrysalis Education Group.

Editor: Elizabeth Neuenfeldt   Designer: Gabriel Hilger

Printed in the United States of America, North Mankato, MN.

TABLE OF CONTENTS

WEATHER THE STORM	4
THE HISTORY OF *FORTNITE*	8
FORTNITE TODAY	16
FORTNITE FANS	20
GLOSSARY	22
TO LEARN MORE	23
INDEX	24

HIGH SCORE
000

WEATHER THE STORM

A player is in a round of *Fortnite*. Their teammate is stuck in the storm. The player rushes back to help them. They use a launchpad. They fly out of the storm!

Fortnite is an online **battle royale game**. It is available on most gaming devices.

People play alone or on teams. They play against up to 99 other players. They battle to be the last person or team standing.

IN-GAME ITEMS

PICKAXE

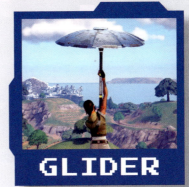
GLIDER

SHIELD POTION

TREASURE CHEST

WOOD

METAL

THE HISTORY OF FORTNITE

FORTNITE: SAVE THE WORLD

Fortnite is made by Epic Games. At first, it was a **survival game**. It was called *Fortnite: Save the World*. Players played **co-op**. The game came out in **early access** in July 2017. But some people did not like it.

A LONG HISTORY

Fortnite was first shown in 2011. But the game was delayed. It was not released until 2017.

DEVELOPER PROFILE

NAME	Epic Games
LOCATION	Cary, North Carolina, United States
YEAR FOUNDED	1991
NUMBER OF EMPLOYEES	around 4,300 in 2023

9

In September 2017, Epic Games released *Fortnite: Battle Royale*. It used the **looting** and building **mechanics** from *Save The World*.

FREE TO PLAY

Fortnite: Battle Royale and *Fortnite Creative* modes are free to play!

The game was a hit! In two weeks, it had over 10 million players.

In December 2017, *Fortnite* began its second **season**. More seasons followed. They added new items and locations.

Epic Games released its first Battle Pass in Season Two. Players could unlock **cosmetics**. They could earn **V-Bucks**.

V-BUCKS

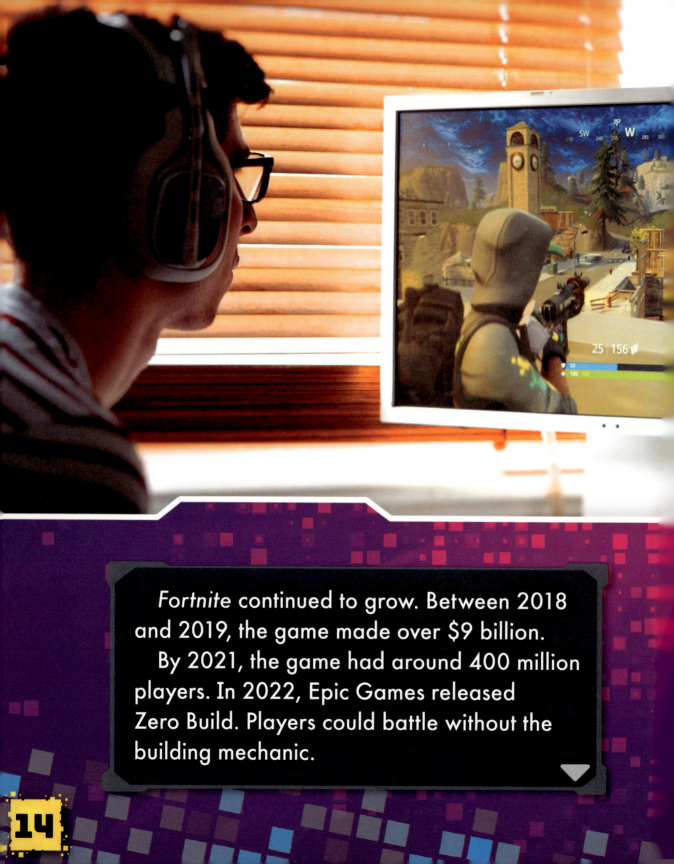

Fortnite continued to grow. Between 2018 and 2019, the game made over $9 billion.
By 2021, the game had around 400 million players. In 2022, Epic Games released Zero Build. Players could battle without the building mechanic.

FORTNITE TIMELINE

July 2017
Fortnite: Save the World comes out in early access

September 2017
Fortnite: Battle Royale is released

December 2017
The first Battle Pass is released

2021
Fortnite has around 400 million players

2022
Zero Build is released

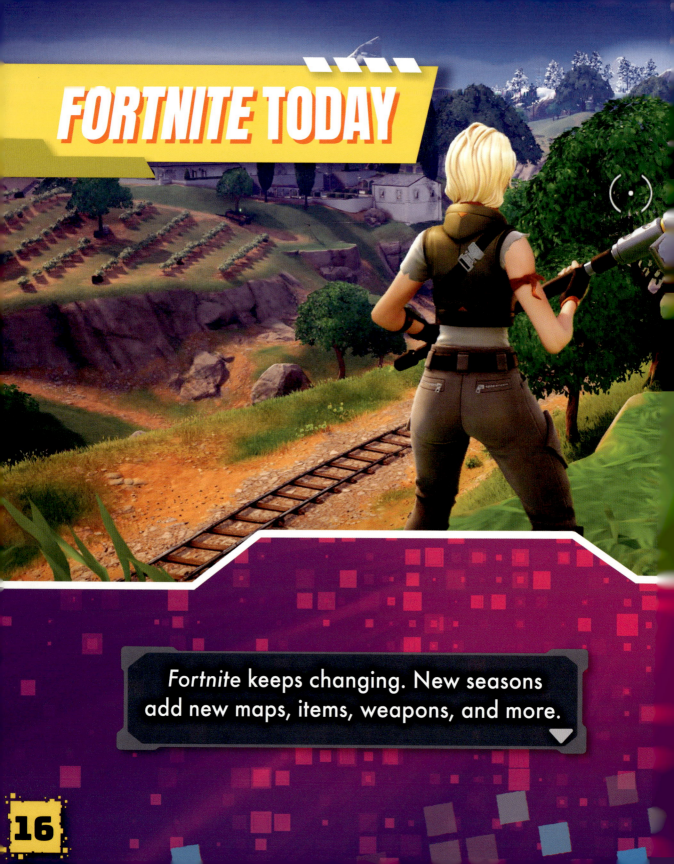

FORTNITE TODAY

Fortnite keeps changing. New seasons add new maps, items, weapons, and more.

LEGO FORTNITE

FORTNITE FESTIVAL

Players can play with or without building. Special event game modes let players enjoy the game in many different ways!

Fortnite features many **crossover** events. The game adds things from different movies, shows, and video games.

MOST USED SKINS IN THE GAME IN 2023

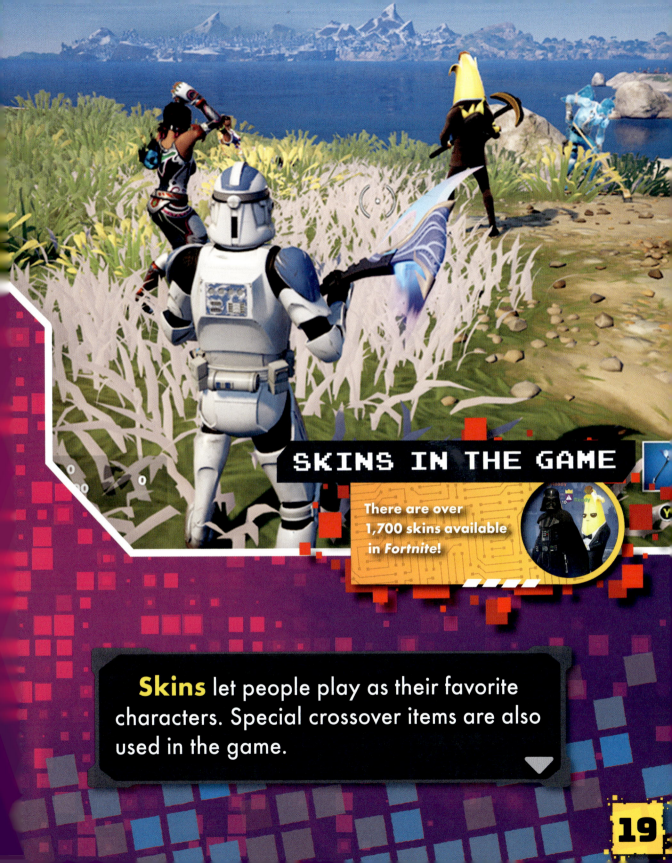

SKINS IN THE GAME

There are over 1,700 skins available in *Fortnite*!

Skins let people play as their favorite characters. Special crossover items are also used in the game.

19

FORTNITE FANS

Fortnite sometimes hosts **virtual** concerts for fans. Fans can also meet up at events. Fortnite players play for the Victory Royale. Skilled players may play in **tournaments**!

FORTNITE WORLD CUP FINAL

DATE 2019

LOCATION New York, New York

EVENT the largest Fortnite tournament to ever take place

20

GLOSSARY

battle royale game—a type of game in which many players compete to be the last player or team standing

co-op—related to working together with other players

cosmetics—visual changes to a game

crossover—related to a joining of two different types of entertainment into one event

early access—a trial version of a game before the full game is released

looting—relating to collecting items in a video game that increase a player's powers or improve their abilities

mechanics—the details of the way something works in a video game

season—a division of time in a video game in which new things are available to players

skins—items that change the appearance of characters in a game

survival game—a type of game in which players have to collect items and fight enemies to stay alive

tournaments—series of games or contests that make up competitions

V-Bucks—a type of money used to buy things in *Fortnite*

virtual—taking place online rather than in the real world

TO LEARN MORE

AT THE LIBRARY
Epic Games. *Fortnite (Official): The Ultimate Locker: The Visual Encyclopedia*. New York, N.Y.: Little, Brown and Company, 2020.

Neuenfeldt, Elizabeth. *Video Games*. Minneapolis, Minn.: Bellwether Media, 2023.

Rathburn, Betsy. *Video Game Developer*. Minneapolis, Minn.: Bellwether Media, 2023.

ON THE WEB

FACTSURFER

Factsurfer.com gives you a safe, fun way to find more information.

1. Go to www.factsurfer.com.

2. Enter "Fortnite" into the search box and click 🔍.

3. Select your book cover to see a list of related content.

INDEX

Battle Pass, 13

battle royale game, 6

building, 10, 14, 17

cosmetics, 13

crossover, 18, 19

Epic Games, 8, 9, 10, 13, 14

event game modes, 17

fans, 20

Fortnite: Battle Royale, 10

Fortnite Creative, 10

Fortnite: Save the World, 8, 10

Fortnite World Cup Final, 20

history, 8, 9, 10, 11, 12, 13, 14, 15

in-game items, 7

items, 12, 16, 19

launchpad, 4

looting, 10

players, 4, 6, 8, 11, 13, 14, 17, 19, 20

season, 12, 13, 16

skins, 18, 19

storm, 4

survival game, 8

timeline, 15

tournaments, 20

V-Bucks, 13

Victory Royale, 20

virtual concerts, 20

Zero Build, 14

The images in this book are reproduced through the courtesy of: steamXO, front cover (*Fortnite* character); Whelsko, front cover (*Fortnite* world); craftnfun, p. 3; Frame Stock Footage, p. 4; Gabriel Hilger, pp. 4-5 (into the storm), 5 (inset), 6-7 (victory), 7 (pickaxe, glider, shield potion, treasure chest, wood, metal), 9 (*Fortnite*), 10 (free to play), 12-13, 13 (V-Bucks), 15 (July 2017, September 2017, December 2017, 2022), 16-17 (*Fortnite*), 17 (*Lego Fortnite*, *Fortnite Festival*); Kieran Downs, pp. 8 (*Fortnite: Save the World*), 15 (2021), 18-19, 19 (skins in the game); Michael Moloney, p. 8 (a long history); Sergey Galyonkin/ Wikipedia, p. 9 (Epic Games headquarters); JJFaq, pp. 10-11; Lenscap Photography, pp. 11, 14-15; dennizn/ Alamy, p. 13 (battle pass); Benedikt Wenck/picture-alliance/dpa/ AP Images, p. 20 (*Fortnite* World Cup Final); Neilson Barnard/ Staff/ Getty Images, pp. 20-21; Sean P. Aune, p. 23.